T

H

E

M

I

N

I

GRAHAM SCOTT
introduced by JOHN COOPER

THE MINI

A CELEBRATION

CHANCELLOR
PRESS

Half-title page: Mid-Sixties club racing Mini.

Title spread: Mini brochures old and new.

First published in 1992 by Hamlyn
This edition published by Chancellor Press in 1997,
an imprint of Reed International Books,
Michelin House, 81 Fulham Road, London SW3 6RB

A catalogue record for this book is available from the British Library

ISBN 1 85152 547 5

Produced by Mandarin Offset

Printed in China

"MINI" is a Trade Mark of the Rover Group Limited
and is registered in many countries of the world.

Editor: John Bailie

Art Editor: Leigh Jones

Picture Researcher: Julia Pashley

The publishers wish to thank John Cooper, the Rover Group, the British Motor Industry
Heritage Trust, and Denise McCluggage for their kind assistance and for providing access to
archive material and information in the production of this book.

ACKNOWLEDGEMENTS
The publishers would like to thank the following organizations and
individuals for their kind permission to reproduce the photographs in
this book:

AutoWeek: /Jack Finucan 51 top
British Film Institute: /United Artists Corporation © 1976 23 top
British Motor Industry Heritage Trust : 2 top right, centre, bottom left and
bottom right, 10, 11, 12, 13 top left and top right, centre, bottom right, 16
top left, 24, 25 bottom left, 27 centre, 28 bottom, 29 bottom left and bottom right, 32 bottom, 35 top right, 38 bottom, 39 top, 41, 42 top left, 43
top left, 45, 54 top left, 54 centre, 54 bottom right, 58, 59 top, 60 bottom
left, 60-1, 61 top left, 61 centre, 62 top left, 69, 71
Neill Bruce: 49 bottom left, 60 top right, 64 top /Peter Roberts Collection
18, 32-3, 34, 34-5, 35 top left, 36, 46 centre left, centre, centre right, 47
top, centre left, centre and centre right, 49 bottom right, 55, 59 bottom, 70
John Cooper: 3 bottom left and bottom right, 6, 7, 29 centre, 38 top left,
46 top, 79
Ronald Grant: /National Screen Service Ltd. 22 top
Chris Harvey: /Mary Harvey 16-7, 25 bottom right, 40, 43 centre right, 52
bottom, 60 centre, 63 bottom right
Haymarket Publishing: 42 top right, 44, 48 bottom, 51 centre, 54 bottom
left, 68, 76 bottom, John Colley 78 top

Norman Hodson: 73 bottom
Bengt Ason Holm Collection: 2 top right, 63 top left and top right
Leigh Jones: 1/2 title page
Hulton Picture Company: 20 centre
Impact Photos: /David Reed 27 bottom right
Mike Key: 50-1, 51 bottom, /Andy Sanders 67 top and bottom
Linda McCartney: 20 bottom
Denise McCluggage: 15 centre, 15 bottom, 33 bottom
Andrew Morland: 8, 28 top, 57, 60 top left, 64 bottom, 64-5, 73 top
National Motor Museum: 14 top, 15 top, 19, 36-7, 52-3, 66 top
Pictorial Press: 23 bottom, 26
Quadrant: 14 bottom, 21 centre, 21 bottom, 22-3, 25 top, 27 top, 27 bot-
tom left, 31, 38 top right, 39 bottom, 42-3, 43 top right, 47 bottom, 56, 61
top right, 62 top right, 63 bottom left, 73 centre /Auto Express 72 top
Rex Features: 20-1, 66 centre and bottom
Rover UK: 3 bottom centre, 9, 13 bottom left, 54 top right, 72 bottom left
and bottom right, 77, 78 bottom
Rover Group, France: 3 top right, 74, 75
Rover Group, Japan: 3 top left, 76 top,
Graham Scott: 65 bottom
Colin Taylor Productions: 30, 43 bottom, 48 left, 48-9, 51 top centre, 52
top, 61 bottom right

CONTENTS

MINI
INTRODUCTION
by JOHN COOPER

Whenever I think of the Mini I think of Sir Alec Issigonis – there would not have been one without the other. We first met in 1946 when we were both competing in the Brighton Speed Trials (I won), and we went on to work very closely together. I have always had a great respect for the man's design capabilities, right from his work on the Morris Minor, which was a very clever design.

We owe a great deal to Sir Alec, because he proved that a small passenger car could have an east-west front-wheel drive engine configuration, which everyone has copied since. His idea of a small car was marvellous but without Jack Daniels the Mini would not have been the success it has been. As an engineer, he kept Sir Alec on the right path.

When the Mini was launched we were already using its A-series engine in our Formula Junior single-seater racing cars, and that racing programme went on to enable Jackie Stewart to win the Formula Three World Championship. When we developed the engine in the Mini to become the Cooper S series we won the British Saloon Car Championship, the European Touring Car Championship and the European Rally Championship outright. Plus we won the Monte Carlo Rally four times, although we were disqualified once. Many of our engines were built by Eddie Maher at Morris Engines, and he did a fantastic job.

During that time I had a wonderful relationship with BMC – we used to just shake hands and get on with the work. During the Seventies I thought it had all ended, and I never dreamed that it would all come back. Now it is just like the Sixties again. Everyone at Rover, including Geoff Pettit, is so enthusiastic that it is just like the old days with BMC, which is wonderful. I've gone 30 years and it's happening all over again.

I am happy to write the introduction to a book that celebrates the sheer fun and adventure that have always been there alongside the successes on rallies and road races. It is incredible that the story is still going on, but I think the Mini will still be with us until at least the end of the century. And for that we have to thank Sir Alec Issigonis, to whom we owe so much. I just wish that he was still with us so that we could tell him.

John Cooper

Left: John Cooper with Sir Alec Issigonis by the Lightweight Special that Sir Alec raced in the Forties.
Above: The Cooper showroom in Surbiton with a Formula Junior (foreground). The single-seater racer was the first to develop the A-series engine that went on to win so many races in Mini Coopers.

CHAPTER I

THE ISSIGONIS DREAM

EVERYONE HAS A DREAM, NO MATTER HOW HUMBLE. A TALENTED ENGINEER WITH THE BRITISH MOTOR CORPORATION IN THE FIFTIES HAD A DREAM THAT A SMALL CAR WOULD BE PUT OUTSIDE THE COTTAGE OF EVERY WORKING MAN. THE CAR THAT ALEC (LATER SIR ALEC) ISSIGONIS DESIGNED EVENTUALLY STOOD OUTSIDE EVERYTHING FROM A PALACE TO A HOVEL. WITH A LIMITED BUDGET, OFTEN SKETCHING ENGINEERING PLANS ON THE BACKS OF ENVELOPES, ISSIGONIS AND HIS CLOSE-KNIT TEAM WORKED AGAINST THE CLOCK TO GET THE CAR IN PRODUCTION. SIR ALEC DIED IN 1988, BUT HIS CAR LIVES ON.

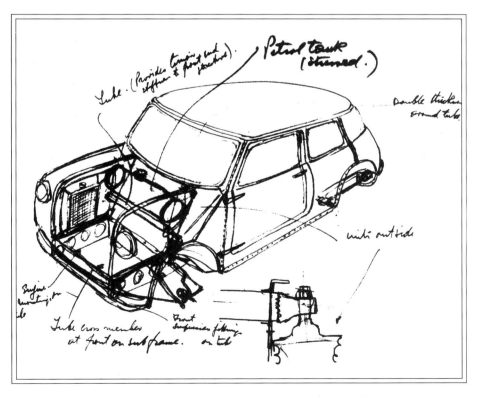

Left: The first production Austin Seven Mini built 4th May 1959.
Above: an early Issigonis sketch shows the side-mounted radiator. The petrol tank located behind the engine was moved to the rear luggage compartment as the design progressed.

The Second World War began in 1939, but its knock-on effects can be felt to this day. Before untold millions died, Adolf Hitler demanded a 'people's car', a 'Volkswagen', that could be bought and run by ordinary 'volk'. The Volkswagen Beetle duly appeared and is still in production, giving lots of pleasure to untold millions as they have tried to work on an overheating, air-cooled engine stuck in the boot.

After the war it was a simple matter to pick up a Tiger tank, but car production took time to recover from the ravages of bombers, either as a result of the damage their bomb-loads caused to factories or because the factories themselves had been turned over to making these destructive monsters. Prewar car design had to suffice in most cases, since people needed transport more than they needed the latest piece of technical wizardry. It was not an auspicious time, and Europe was still far from recovery when the Suez crisis arrived. Once again Britain was plunged into gloom: fuel rationing and horrid little cars designed by horrid little men appeared.

Every engineer wanted to burst the bubble cars that were popping out of Germany, and nowhere was this feeling stronger than at British Motor Corporation in Birmingham. The company didn't really want to follow the trend and build bubble cars, but resources were relatively few and the budget remarkably tight, so it was a situation that called for imagination and flair to cover up the material deficiencies. The task of finding a new car that used the minimum of materials for the maximum amount of space was eventually given to Alec Issigonis in 1957. Issigonis had led an itinerant existence after being brought up in Smyrna (Izmir), an area at times owned by the Greeks, at times by the Turks. His family had a good business making boilers, but it was with the internal combustion engine that Alec was to make his name. He came to England and worked in the motor trade until he found a niche at Morris, a few years before the Second World War. There, in the late 1940s, he designed the first British car to sell a million – the Morris Minor.

About a decade later Leonard Lord, company chairman of BMC, wanted him to produce a smaller version of the same vehicle, but Issigonis had his own ideas. Then again, he had to deal with a company chairman, rather than the Führer. He knew that if he was to build the best small car he would have to do better than copy others on the market. He would also have to break new engineering ground if the car and four adults were to occupy little space on the road. To build this small car he had a small budget, a small time frame and a small team, but he thought big.

Issigonis and his design team of eight men decided on front-wheel drive to save the space taken up by the transmission. Tests were conducted with a two-cylinder engine but it was far too rough and gutless and was instantly discarded. This left a traditional four-cylinder engine and, with the pace of development and limited budget, there was no alternative but to go

Above: Nearly there: 1957 prototype XC9003 is the right shape and size but still has the front grille to be designed.

Below: Pre-production engine; production cars had the engine turned round with the carburettor at the rear to prevent icing-up, placing the distributor at the front - which is why early cars used to cut out in the rain! The battery was moved to the boot to improve weight distribution.

Right: Cut-away shows how compact is the design; note how the rear suspension leaves the boot space free.

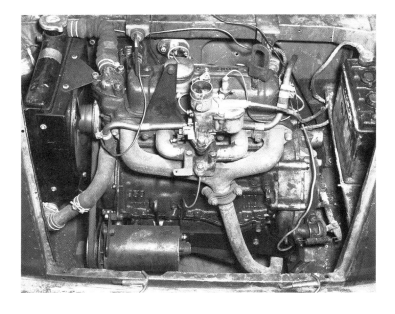

shopping for something already on the shelf. Into the shopping basket went the Morris Minor A-series engine. This was not a bad engine but Issigonis had wanted to replace it in the Minor several years before, so it was simply a 'make do' lump that everyone hoped would one day be replaced by something radically better. We are still waiting for that day more than 30 years later.

The goal was to have a car about ten feet long, but this cannot be done if the four-cylinder engine is going to stick out the front. The only way is to turn it sideways, which is what Issigonis did. But in a car only four feet two inches wide the engine with its attendant gearbox is too long to fit in the space available, if you feel it might be a good idea to have some steering movement. Problem! Issigonis took the decision, with time running out, to mount the gearbox under the engine, which hadn't been tried before. It worked. (Front-wheel drive and a transverse engine had been used on a two-cylinder DKW as far back as 1931.)

As he grappled with the particular demands of zero space, Issigonis must have dreamed of his time in the 1950s when he worked for Alvis, designing a big 3.5-litre V8 sports saloon, with loads of room to fit everything. That car, which never saw production, had rubber suspension, which was the medium he employed for the new car since it was cheap and effective without taking up too much space or weight. Obviously, in such a light car, the weight of four adults represented a significant variable, even if the slender Twiggy was soon to become the role model.

Left: Classic rear suspension design by Alex Moulton. Rubber was used instead of the usual springs to overcome the harsh ride caused by the tiny 10-inch wheels.
Right: A bare body-shell waiting to be sprayed shows the monocoque design, at a time when most cars had separate chassis and body.

It was vital that the suspension system should be effective, because there was going to be less suspension work done by the tyres, which were, inevitably, small. Issigonis had horrified engineers by demanding wheel rims of only about eight inches, although they later compromised on ten inches. There was a sharp intake of breath among the professionals while engineers considered the problems of high temperature and wear associated with tiny tyres – and where would the brakes go? Dunlop took up the challenge, since their tyres were going to be original equipment and they had a close working relationship with BMC. They had to work fast, against a background of prophecies of doom from their German counterparts since motorways had just opened in West Germany and the little bubble cars were forever blowing tyres on them. But in England, in 1958, there were no motorways to worry about or test on, since Motorway One was not to open for another year.

Time, space and money: these factors frustrated the design team throughout 1958 and early 1959. There was so little money that they couldn't even build the cars up on jigs, which is why Minis have seams, which are spot-welded jigging ribs, done to save money. Issigonis mockingly called himself an 'odd ironmonger' but he drove his team on with inspired answers to every problem. Often he wouldn't be able to communicate his thoughts clearly, so he tended to scribble frantically on the backs of envelopes, bits of scrap paper – anything that came to hand. These free-hand drawings would be taken away and redrawn by designers, who would often find the answer they were looking for on the back of a gas bill.

The engine continued to give trouble, even though it proved extremely fast. The clutch was slipping because of oil spray and the carburettor was prone to icing up, but to every problem Issigonis found at least

a partial solution. The answer to the carburettor was a radical one so late in the day: they turned the engine round through 180 degrees. This got the carburettor safely positioned above the exhaust manifold, behind the main block, curing that particular problem, but the extra gearing necessary slowed the car down. Since it didn't rain much during testing nobody worried unduly that the distributor was now right at the front of the engine, all but open to the elements. There wasn't time to worry about something until it actually went wrong.

The engine size dropped 100cc to 848cc; the car grew sideways two inches. These two factors took the edge off the performance but nobody worried unduly since it still seemed nippier than the opposition. The launch loomed as spring turned to summer, and the bodywork went through more styling changes than a model on the catwalk. The final body wasn't exactly stunning but it was neat and shapely without being too dumpy. It has been suggested that the rounded, small shape of the Mini brings out the maternal instinct and, who knows, that may be right. The Italian designer Sergio Farina wanted to restyle the car and made the mistake of asking Issigonis. Prophetically, Issigonis replied: 'Look at your cars, they're like women's clothes – out of date in two years. My car will still be in fashion after I've gone.'

However, not a great deal of thought had been given as to who exactly was going to buy this little marvel. The car was eventually launched on 26 August 1959 through both the Austin and Morris franchises around the world. The franchises operated independently, so there was much duplication of effort to herald the arrival of both the Austin Seven and the Morris Mini Minor. It was priced at £496, which was roughly the price of the wrongly named Ford Popular, and nearly £100 cheaper than the Ford Anglia, neither of which were exactly technological masterpieces. At that

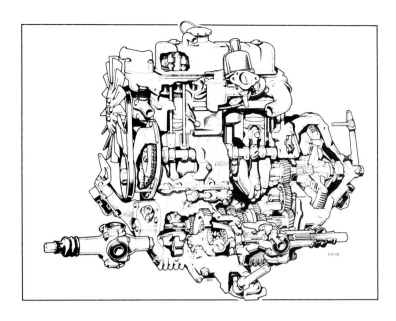

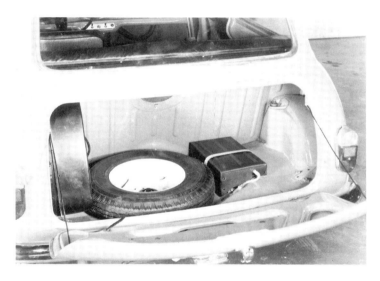

Above: The A-series engine had the gearbox under the engine to save space.

Above right: The spartan interior shows Issigonis's obsession with saving space; note the capacious door bins and large parcel shelf alongside the solitary dial. The floor-mounted ignition button, although convenient, was vulnerable to wet road conditions.

Right: On production cars the battery shared the boot with the spare wheel and the fuel tank. It was not an easy task to replace the battery, having to negotiate the boot-lid whilst leaning in to the restricted space.

Below right: Note the Sixties sucker-type roof rack, the rear window heater element (also sucker mounted), and the tiny reversing light on this export model.

Below: Issigonis at Longbridge in 1965. The white Mini was the very first one off the line six years before.

Left: Early Sixties publicity aimed at young ladies 'travelling light' with the 1962 Morris Mini Super de-luxe. **(inset)** More young ladies demonstrate BMC's emphasis on the carrying capacity. Evident on this very early Austin Seven is the hinged number-plate.

Right: 'I thought *you* had the boy.' The Mini Traveller could carry even more with its longer wheelbase. The wood trim was later dropped on the more basic models.

price BMC weren't just cutting their own throats, they were taking a hot bath and opening every vein in their corporate body.

But at least they got there first. The first winter there were problems with floor sills leaking, and the pungent odour of rotting carpets became a familiar smell to hundreds of owners. Thousands of others had plenty of time to ponder the wisdom of putting the distributor right at the front of the engine when they found themselves stranded at the side of the road every time it rained. Eventually a card sheet was fitted to keep the worst of the rain off, but, compared to some of the more modern horror stories, when manufacturers have used the public as a final Research & Development department, the Mini was relatively untroubled – a tribute to the work carried out under pressure by Issigonis and his sweater-wearing, pipe-

smoking team. Other companies were known to be working on the small car concept, and everyone knew that the first car out, even if not perfect, would pick up the lion's share. The Mini beat the Hillman Imp on to the market by three years and, while the Imp was an interesting car with lots of potential for racers and road drivers alike, the mere fact that it came out later cost its owners, Rootes, around £9 million in lost sales.

The dream of Alec Issigonis, the penniless traveller from a shifting country, was that every worker would have a Mini outside his cottage. It would be cheap and practical and loved and the world would be a better place. What was then called the working class has been the downfall of many. Too many people have been killed or ruined by others championing what they imagine to be the aspirations of the working class. The workers were wary of this little box on wheels and

Below: In a campaign named 'Operation 850', BMC hired a host of stars to introduce the Mini to the United States, including, from left to right: Stirling Moss, Innes Ireland, Pedro Rodriguez, Denise McCluggage and Dickie Thompson. Both Stirling Moss and Innes Ireland managed to roll their Minis.
Right: John Cooper reveals the tiny engine to an astonished five times world champion Juan Fangio. Fangio turned up at Lime Rock to replace Moss who had suffered his F1 career-ending crash back in England at Goodwood. Fangio and protégé Juan Manuel Bordeau sported tam-o'-shanters to add to the British occasion to the amusement of all involved.

Above: It's 1961 and the Coopers are coming, as the first 997 sits in its subframe. The twin SU carburettors, three branch exhaust manifold and other modifications helped raise the power to a dizzy 55bhp. The top speed was 85mph, while the tiny 7-inch Lockheed disc brakes brought things to a halt. The remote control gear shift made it easier to change gear than the earlier, floppy direct lever.

Right: A year later, 1962, and the Coopers sported the distinctive white roofs, as on this fine Austin Cooper example.

declined to put their money into it. This was a pity because the car had been designed with them in mind. The advertising campaigns were run for them, with economy as the main message: 'A penny a mile', declared the advertisements, basing their assertion on the claimed 50mpg. The ads pointed out the front-wheel drive, the giddy 70mph, the 'ride is a glide' of the rubber suspension, the technological perkiness of the package, but the working man is a traditional man, nervous of change or technical innovation, and his money stayed under the bed.

But others had noticed. The Mini was a small, low box with a wheel at each corner and a reasonable engine, a recipe that made it attractive to both tuners and racers. Leading this group was John Cooper, a name as synonymous with the Mini as that of Sir Alec Issigonis. In 1959 and 1960 he was the World Champion Formula One racing car constructor and had had personal success in his 500cc special, at the same time that Issigonis was campaigning his Lightweight Special. His drivers, Jack Brabham and Bruce McLaren, both drove Minis on the road and were wildly enthusiastic about their potential. John Cooper knew all about tuning the A-series since this was the engine in his Formula Junior cars, an engine which came from the Morris plant at Coventry. He discussed with Issigonis the idea of building some specials, but Issigonis was still locked into the idea of the Mini as everyman's transport. Although Issigonis was a business colleague, Cooper felt strongly enough to go over his head to the then chairman of BMC, George Harriman, to ask if he could build a run of four-seater GTs. Nowadays such a request would lose traction in

departmental meetings, skid sideways in Product Planning and go belly up in Accounts, but after a brief meeting Harriman said: 'Yes. Go away and do it!'.

John Cooper remembers: 'Harriman said that we had to make 1000 – but we eventually made 150,000!' The engines had longer bores to take the capacity to 997cc and had twin SU carburettors fitted. The engine was strengthened to cope with the 55bhp these and other changes wrought. The gear ratios were altered and a remote gearchange fitted, designed by John Cooper himself – a boon for those whose knuckles didn't drag along the ground. One of the major

advances, though, was in the braking. Lockheed were intrigued by the thought of getting disc brakes on such tiny wheels and fell for John Cooper's bait. Disc brakes on such a car were a technological marvel, even though the same units now feel like drum brakes compared to the multi-piston calipers in use today. But at the time they made for a safer car on the road and also allowed much later braking in competition.

The first Mini Cooper came out in October 1961, just two years after the launch of the original car, an incredibly short time in design and production terms. The Mini became inseparable from Cooper and

Cooper inseparable from the Mini, even though there was never any official agreement between the two, and Cooper only received a £2 royalty on every car for the Research & Development. That seems ridiculous now, but it was a time of optimism, when anything seemed possible. Indeed, for the Mini Coopers anything was possible. Although Issigonis hadn't designed the Mini with the race track and rally route in mind it must have satisfied his 'small is beautiful' philosophy to find that he had created a giant killer. Ahead lay more than a decade of competition and success both on the track and the showroom floor. Ahead lay the Sixties.

MINI

MINI SKIRTS MINI CARS

THE LITTLE CAR DROVE INTO A REVOLUTION. IN THE SIXTIES THE BARRIERS OF CLASS AND MONEY WERE UNDER ATTACK AS NEVER BEFORE, AND THE MINI PROVED A PERFECT WEAPON IN THE BATTLE FOR EQUALITY. DRIVEN BY PRINCESSES AND HARLOTS, POP STARS AND BARONETS, THE MINI BECAME A VITAL FASHION ACCESSORY IN THE STYLE CAPITAL OF THE WORLD. LONDON'S CARNABY STREET AND KING'S ROAD WERE THE STAGE ON WHICH MINIS AND THEIR OWNERS STRUTTED AND POSED, THE CARS ADORNED WITH LUSTROUS PAINT, COUNTLESS ACCESSORIES AND WITH INTERIORS OF SUMPTUOUS LUXURY.

'Damn Minis, damn Mini-skirts!'

Left: The MkII Mini was introduced in 1967 with the Super de-luxe 1000. Mini owners were also growing up and becoming more sophisticated.
Above: Cartoons about the Mini spoke for themselves.

He was not a radical – 'I am an engineer' he used to explain. When he retired as Sir Alec Issigonis he lived in a quiet bungalow in Birmingham with a Mini parked outside. His life was a far cry from the lifestyle that his car helped to create. The Mini went to parties, got filled with students and marijuana smoke, got caught up in protest riots and was seen in all the best places with all the fab and groovy folk. The Min was in.

The Swinging Sixties was undoubtedly the most exciting decade this century, when the young came out from parental control to over-indulge in sex and drugs and rock'n'roll. With jobs and money in plentiful supply anything seemed possible as many of the old barriers came down. There was sexual liberation, female emancipation, equality and jobs for all in a world where the young took control. Maybe that was how it was meant to be, and doubtless some believed it all, but at the end of the decade which started with the Sharpeville Massacre and the rise of the Berlin Wall and which ended with Biafra and The Troubles in Northern Ireland there were only small advances that remained, like the abolition of the death penalty and the introduction of the Pill.

But in the early Sixties that was all in the exciting

future. The main point was that all barriers of class, age and wealth were to be broken down, when earls became dustmen and when street urchins became pop stars. The Mini was perfect. It offered performance, handling and sheer zip to a whole spectrum of people, nearly all of whom were higher up the social ladder than the people the car had been designed for. You didn't need an unobtainable sports car to burn someone off at the lights, you needed an easily affordable Mini. It was cheeky and it was, above all, fun. To have fun and to be seen doing so was essential and never has a car given so much fun per pound note as the Mini. There's something about driving one, the way it turns as fast as you can think, the way it darts through motorbike-sized gaps, the way the gears and exhaust whine and burble as you cut through the traffic – as the sticker said: 'You've just been Mini'd'.

Top: Parisiennes in a Mini Moke derivative designed by someone who had obviously lost his 'French curves'.

Above left: Christine 'Profumo Affair' Keeler and her Mini – enough to tempt even the clergy.

Left: The Yardbirds check it out courtesy of renowned photographer Linda McCartney.

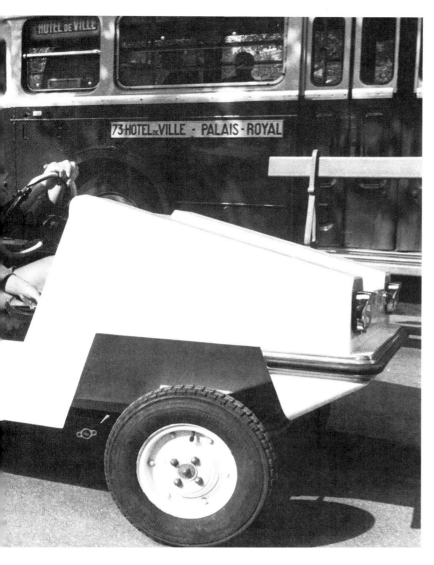

inches long was a vital fashion accessory if you wanted to stay cool. Twenty five years later the Japanese learned the same lesson with the Mini for the same reasons all over again.

At the launch of the Mini eighty cars were given to leading figures for a whole year so that they could 'evaluate' the Mini. This helped to get the car at most of the main social and political functions over the next year, where the press dutifully turned up in their Minis and photographed famous people stepping out of theirs. Marketing in those days was hardly as sophisticated or ruthless as it is today, but when Issigonis took the Queen for a drive round Windsor Park in a Mini it was obvious that the final accolade had been bestowed.

Having a crown ripping the roof lining is highly desirable but in a decade of people power it wasn't really enough. What was needed was for the new meritocracy to signal approval, and this they did with their cheque books. Media stars from singer Lulu to model Twiggy to comedian Spike Milligan were all enthusiastic owners, as were Lord Snowdon and Princess Margaret.

In 1965, when David Bailey married Catherine Deneuve with Mick Jagger as best man, Courrèges loosed the mini-skirt on an unsuspecting world. As the

The English motorway system was in its infancy, in those halcyon days before the M25 Ring of Death enveloped London, so long, fast journeys were not such a part of everyday life as they are now. Traffic was a problem, though, particularly in London, which was the place to be if you were anybody. A cool Saturday afternoon might take in a visit to Mary Quant's clothes shop in the King's Road, Chelsea, then a short drive up to Barbara Hulanicki's Biba shop in Kensington Church Street before driving down to hang out in Carnaby Street to watch the fashion parade on the pavements. You could hardly be cool if you were stuck in traffic or sweatily trying to squeeze into a tiny parking slot, so a Mini proved the perfect vehicle. This was in the days before parking bays were marked out, bays which take account of large cars, so anything that could be parked in a gap only 11 feet 6

Above right: The record of how many students could fit in a Mini stands at 24. It's always fun trying to beat it, but can also be a health risk!

Right: This patriotically painted Austin Mini was prepared at the Longbridge plant for the Montreal World Fair in 1967. It was also used for an attempt on the above record as part of its publicity campaign.

Above: The film *The Italian Job* featured Michael Caine, Noel Coward, E-Type Jaguars, a Lamborghini Miura and an Aston Martin, but it was a troupe of flying Minis that stole the show. **Right:** This Mini was built for Ringo Starr by Radford, with an opening tailgate to accommodate his drums. Peter Sellers pioneered the concept so that, he claimed, he could carry portly fellow Goon, Harry Secombe around.

Sixties progressed the skirt lengths became ever shorter until Customs officials had to start measuring dress bust size as well as hemline length to determine whether the garment was liable for women's or children's purchase tax. As dry cleaners started charging to clean mini-skirts by the inch many foresaw the collapse of what remained of the empire into chaos. But the young took to the mini-skirt in the same way as the Mini car, the two going together in a fairly eye-boggling combination. Motoring magazines of the time even had features, purportedly written by women, on the problems of getting into and, especially, out of Minis while wearing mini-skirts. Jean 'The Shrimp' Shrimpton was championing both mini-skirts and Mini cars in the year that 'Time' magazine ran the headline: '1966: The Year of Swinging London'.

But, needless to say in this decade of equality, it didn't take long before some people wanted their Mini to be different to the next. Actor Peter Sellers led the charge in what he thought was an inimitable way – but it wasn't long before he was imitated. In London sheer performance wasn't really required, but what was essential was a look that would turn heads. This was a time of people power, when individual whims could be indulged. In an earlier decade a comedian would have received a frosty reception by the glacial assistants at H R Owen, a name more synonymous with Rolls-Royce, if he had dared to ask for a frivolous conversion for his car, but this was the Sixties and it was a

Sellers market. He went to H R Owen, who in turn went to a coachbuilders called Hooper, for a really wacky idea: wickerwork side panels. Hooper, who built probably the best Rolls-Royce bodies ever, did a marvellous job, but automotive jokes were not for them and they left the idea up to others to emulate. Soon such side panels were all the rage and Sellers moved on to other ideas. Deep in The Goons, he had a company called Radford make another Mini with an opening tailgate – he claimed it was so that Harry Secombe could come along.

Before long the specialists, the coachbuilders, the seat makers, were moving in on the Mini and its rich owners, taking the basic box further and further away from the dream of Issigonis. Radford, having had a flying start with Peter Sellers, produced more and more sumptuous Minis, until the lucky owner was all but sitting in a small box full of cotton wool. (This at a time when an accepted cure for the perpetually rattling gear lever was to strap a length of garden hose over it to cure the vibration.) The Radford seats and trim grew thick with leather, the wooden dashboard glittered with dials while the floor grew so deep with

foam, felt and carpet that it was a positive effort to press down on the accelerator. The humble Min became the Cooper Mini de Ville Grand Luxe, with a price tag to match of £1100. By 1967 the Radford Mini de Ville MkIII was £3000 more expensive than a base model 850 but the list of extras was endless: twin speakers, electric windows, automatic reversing light, hazard flashers, sun roof, seat belts, self-parking wipers and electric screen washers. An amazing list for the time, but now all those extras come as standard on most modern cars.

Two men, Wood and Pickett, left Radford to start their own business in cosseting Minis, and soon picked up an order from Peter Sellers who wanted a car built for Britt Ekland. They had 'stock' models, like the Margrave, but their speciality was doing made-to-order specials. Wood and Pickett beavered away at the market until they struck gold, or oil to be precise,

Below: The Pink Panther film *A Shot In The Dark* featured Peter Sellers, who also dreamt up the wacky wickerwork side panels.
Bottom: Margrave Minis were built by Wood and Pickett; some, like this one, had Mercedes headlamps.

when Arab oil money moved in during the 1970s. With essentials like telephone, television, air-conditioning, electric sun-roof and quadraphonic hi-fi, the little Mini now cost something like £20,000, somewhat more than the £496 of 15 years before.

The factory never really got onto the bandwagon, but the Cooper Car Company was sufficiently intrigued to commission Bertone, the Italian styling house, to come up with an executive Mini. The result was the Cooper S VIP, but it never went into production. It was left to the small specialists to transform the worker's wheels into a pampered palace that was once again miles beyond his reach. The joke of the wickerwork sidepanels was a good one, but it's hard to see who had the last laugh.

But if these creations were unattainable, there was still plenty that the ordinary man or student could do to tart up the stock box. Issigonis took a rather personal view of Mini design and, since he didn't like car radios or seat belts, he simply didn't build them into the original car. Needless to say, these were among the first items fitted, but the addition of seat belts threw up another problem. If you wore them like a law-abiding citizen you couldn't reach the gear lever or the switches, a problem exacerbated by the fact that inertia reel belts were not yet around. Gear and switch extensions soon appeared along with seat and steering wheel extensions for those tall people for whom the Mini was a contortionist's nightmare. With the Riley Elf getting into production a couple of companies even made fibreglass boot extensions, for those who prized space above aesthetics.

The main point was not what you could alter but what you could add. Rests there were aplenty, for arm, leg and head, and badge bars, nudge bars and boot bars. Everything from slick Peco exhausts to Fiamm

air horns to horn rings went on, under, in or round the luckless Mini, which ended up with more useless toys than Santa Claus. However, there was one essential extra, without which your Mini simply would not run properly: a striped tiger's tail, priced one shilling, from all Esso garages.

Throughout the decade the Mini moved on, in 850, 1000, Clubman, 997 Cooper, Cooper S, and 1275GT guise, as well as the estate Travellers and the Countrymen, which had wooden supports at the rear which were decorative (and expensive) rather than functional. The racing successes of the Sixties had a knock-on effect not just on would-be rally drivers. Extra spotlights, Paddy Hopkirk heel-and-toe throttle and brake lever kits and dinky little steering wheels found their way onto many high street cruisers, who were simply spoiled for choice for extras from the disparate worlds of fashion and racing and rallying. The Mini simply wasn't big enough to fit them all on.

But for those of a gentler persuasion there were some practical extras. The Mini was one of the earliest cars to appeal strongly to women, who found the dumpy little thing friendly and accessible – apart from the problem of wearing a mini-skirt in one. By 1978 50 per cent of all Minis were bought by women, who had been buying them in increasing numbers since the Sixties. There was obviously a danger of falling between the twin demands of women drivers and male boy racers, but the image of Fun satisfied both parties. There wasn't any particular reason why fun should be uncomfortable, so in 1964 Issigonis introduced Hydrolastic suspension, which was more comfortable than the previous rubber ride, but also more expensive. It was gone by 1971. With Hydrolastic, front and rear suspension pitch is balanced by a fluid connection but in practice the result could be a bit like floating

Top: A 1966 Austin Mini Super de-luxe Mk1 casts a long shadow.

Above: The Riley Elf (left) and the Wolseley Hornet (right) were partially successful attempts by BMC to boot the Mini up-market.

Left: Badge engineering gone berserk. The 1968-9 range, with badges from Austin, Morris, Wolseley and Riley. The commercial vans pre-dated the wood-framed estates by about seven months, with the pick-ups, also based on the longer wheelbase, following a little later.

Above: The Mini soon created its own accessory industry and car magazines of the day were full of adverts like these. The Peco exhausts are still produced to the same pattern, and the Minifin drum brakes remain very popular.

Left: The Poster Motor Company turned Minis into mobile advertisements during the Seventies. Companies gained publicity and the owners got some revenue and, at the end of it, a free re-spray.

Right: The Clubman of 1970 was far uglier than its predecessor — Clubfoot would have been a better name.

Below: The Mini 1275GT Clubman lacked both the performance and the charisma of the Cooper. Owners had to supply their own.

Right: Jenny Agutter with her rather anonymous Mini — even film stars need anonymity from time to time. Nudge bars were an essential part of living in traffic - congested cities such as London or Paris.

Below: The components of the automatic gearbox.

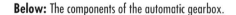
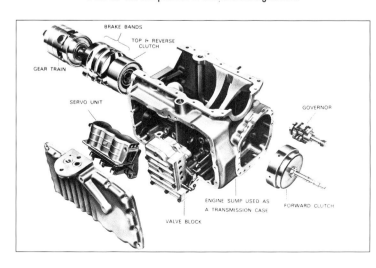

down the Channel. Jerky movement was replaced by a sea-roll as the front rose and fell, less hard on the body but far from perfect for the average landlubber.

Automatic transmission worked rather better, arriving a year after the Hydrolastic suspension. Working in conjunction with Automotive Products, BMC came up with a neat four-speed auto gearbox, which was something of a marvel and a milestone in

Above and left: The 1964 1275 Mini Cooper S. This was the Cooper to have, the heir to a continuous homologation programme to keep the Mini competitive on the racetrack and in rallies.

Top right: John Cooper and friends in Bayonne, France, for the opening of a new dealer. This Downton Mini was prepared by Daniel Richmond, one of the experts on extracting horsepower.

Below left: It takes one to catch one ... The police used the Mini Cooper S. Although not really suitable on the motorway, it would have been ideal for chasing the Jaguars of bank robbers in the cities.

Below right: Home on the range? A wolf in wolf's clothing...

such a small, cramped engine. Naturally some power was lost in the conversion, about ten per cent, but for those not in a hurry or of a terminally lazy disposition it was perfect. It also got round the problem of not being able to reach the original gearstick if you wore a seat belt. Enzo Ferrari owned at least three Minis, which he used to drive up in the hills purely for enjoyment. BMC made him an automatic version and drove it out there – only to find when they got there that they hadn't thought to convert it to left-hand drive, and Enzo gracefully declined the present.

Anything that made the Mini gentler or more comfortable was often welcome since it must be admitted that it was a far from comfortable ride. Compared to a modern hot hatchback the Mini has a nervy, jagged ride, with uncomfortable seats, very upright driving position, high noise levels and of course a roof problem for anyone vaguely giraffe-like. Issigonis actually theorised that the driver should never be too comfortable in case he lost concentration. (Anyone laughing at that theory might ponder the behaviour of a modern businessman slouched in his leather arm-chair in a cocooned executive express as he sits in the outside lane at 90mph listening to Vivaldi.)

By the end of the decade the Mini didn't look as exciting and sparkling new as it had done in 1960, but at least it was an established part of the landscape. What had seemed technically marvellous was now run-of-the-mill but, then again, eveyone was tired and mostly disillusioned by 1970. Ahead lay a tough decade for everyone, including the increasingly strike-bound and desperate Mini management. The decade had taken its toll, partly because not enough money had been made out of the Mini so not enough was ploughed back into uprating it. Suspension that had seemed comfortable now seemed harsh; performance that had seemed thrilling now seemed pedestrian. But few got out of the Sixties in better shape than they went in. Marilyn Monroe, John Kennedy, Donald Campbell, Brian Epstein, Che Guevara, Martin Luther King, Jim Clark, Bobby Kennedy – all dead by violence or their own hand at the end of the decade of love and peace. The Mini, the Sixties icon, passed two million sales in 1969 and survived them all.

RED BRICK RALLYING

THE MOUNTAIN FASTNESS LIES SILENT UNDER SNOW. THE HARSH TRACK IS LIT BY HEADLAMPS, WAVERING AND DARTING AS THEY APPROACH. WITH A THROATY BURBLE A RED MINI SLIDES INTO VIEW - A TINY THING AGAINST SUCH A BACKDROP. ITS WHEELS SCRABBLE FOR GRIP ON THE ICY SURFACE AS THE DRIVER THROWS THE CAR SIDEWAYS; A BUSTLING RED BRICK IN A BLEAK, WHITE LANDSCAPE. ROCKS SCOUR THE UNDERBELLY OF THE CAR AS IT CLATTERS AND CAREERS DOWN THE TRACK, RUSHING HEADLONG TO THE WARMTH AND SOPHISTICATION OF MONTE CARLO. IT WILL LOOK OUT OF PLACE, BUT IT WILL WIN.

Left: The classic image of a red-hot Mini hurtling through the snows to Monte Carlo. Timo Makinen on the 1967 rally, which was won by team-mate Rauno Aaltonen.
Above: This is the engine of Tony Fall's 1966-67 rally mount GRX 195D; 1275cc and just 70bhp.

The phrase 'racing improves the breed' might have been invented for the Mini. During the 1960s the factory also discovered that racing improves the profits. The Mini moved into the public consciousness not as an image of a practical little box in the suburbs but as a screaming, foglamped red brick hurtling through the air on the way to Monte Carlo.

Minis got the chequered flag in virtually every type of competition but it was in rallying that the gallant little car gained most fame and fortune. In the Sixties one of the main aims of rallying was to show the strength and endurance of what you could buy in the showroom. Having a one-off wonder winning everything was not seen as a successful marketing campaign. A Paris-Dakar winning Peugeot T16 is a stunning package of technology, right at the forefront of engineering and electronics development, but the average car buyer is going to see through the advertising hype and know perfectly well that a T16 has virtually nothing to do with the Peugeot 205 in the garage. On the other hand a Mini seen winning a rally one year was likely to have some positive benefits on the showroom model the following year, and everyone knew that the showroom floor was where the car had originated from in the first place.

Right: Paddy Hopkirk chases an evil-handling VW on the 1963 RAC Rally. What is the piece of paper the VW driver is holding – his will?

Below: Winners of the *Coupe des Dames* on the 1962 Monte Carlo Rally; Ann Wisdom and driver Pat Moss. Ann and Pat, sister of Stirling, were also the first women to win an international rally, when they triumphed in the Tulip Rally the same year.

A low centre of gravity and a wheel at each corner meant that fine handling was the Mini's greatest asset. Steering was fast and precise, braking fine, and handling exemplary with the independent rubber suspension. When Minis switched over to the Hydrolastic suspension many competitors simply ran the car down on the bump-stops anyway, so its pitching motion wasn't too much of a problem.

But the front-engine, front-wheel drive configuration did result in a new handling trait – understeer. Enthusiastic drivers soon discovered that hammering into a corner started to push the front wheels out, towards oncoming traffic or the far verge. Until the advent of the Mini, people were used to oversteer building up, with the tail of the car coming round if too much enthusiasm overcame too little rubber. It was a new problem in rallying as well as on the road, but on the off-tracks Scandinavian drivers provided a new answer – left-foot braking.

Braking itself could be mildly hazardous for those used to more weight in the rear, since the positioning of the engine right over the front wheels, allied to very light weight, meant that heavy braking put tremendous pressure on the front of the car but made the rear feather-light. As a result most of the work on disc brakes went into the front pair, since big brakes on the rear would inevitably mean locked rear wheels every time the driver punched the middle pedal.

But none of this was of any use until more horsepower was extracted from the A-series engine. Aerodynamics were not exactly a strong point – a barn door probably has a lower drag coefficient – so the only way to go faster was to extract more power out of the elderly engine. John Cooper had had plenty of experience exploiting the A-series for his Formula Junior single-seater racers, so his Mini Coopers were fast and well engineered. The 997 was first, followed by 998, 1071S, 970S, and 1275S versions, as part of a ten-year agreement signed in 1961.

But to win races you need more than a car. In the early Sixties the BMC competition department at Abingdon had a team committed to getting the Mini past the chequered flag first. This is in the days before cars became 'units', before a British car could have a Japanese engine, panels stamped in Spain and electrics put together in France. BMC was big but it wasn't as faceless as a conglomerate today and it was, damn it all, British.

The manager of the works teams was Stuart Turner, who went on to head Ford's competition drive. An aggressive ex-competitor, he handled both the tactics and the strategy of the teams with matchless efficiency and cunning. Engine preparation was entrusted to Downton, a Wiltshire-based tuning business run by Daniel Richmond, a meticulous engineer who realized the potential locked into the Mini very early on. Sadly, Richmond died young, at 46, a tragedy that drove his wife to suicide some five years later. But during his working life with the Mini his

Below: American works rally driver Denise McCluggage, with co-driver Rosemary Sears, won the *Coupe des Dames* on the 1963 Alpine Rally.

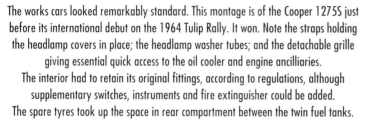

The works cars looked remarkably standard. This montage is of the Cooper 1275S just before its international debut on the 1964 Tulip Rally. It won. Note the straps holding the headlamp covers in place; the headlamp washer tubes; and the detachable grille giving essential quick access to the oil cooler and engine ancilliaries.
The interior had to retain its original fittings, according to regulations, although supplementary switches, instruments and fire extinguisher could be added.
The spare tyres took up the space in rear compartment between the twin fuel tanks.

beautifully prepared engines did much for the trophy cupboard. The rumour was that the engines were in such good condition because Richmond cleaned them with his favourite liquid, Gordon's Gin.

The cars, the management, the engineers were all lined up. What was needed was some drivers. Although the Mini was being rallied almost within minutes of the first ones coming off the production line, the early events inevitably showed up teething troubles, with breakages and breakdowns leading to a slow start. One of the most notable casualties was the original road wheel, since the forces thrust through them regularly broke wheels into pieces. It was John Cooper who designed a stylish and strong replacement, and production of the Minilite wheel continues to this day. With the chance of the wheels falling off the underpowered car, top drivers flocked away from the Mini.

Hard-boy Scandinavians started to switch from front-wheel drive Saabs to front-wheel drive Minis but it was a woman who gave the Mini its first international present. Pat Moss, sister of Stirling, was one of the top rally drivers in the early Sixties, originally driving big Healeys before switching to the Mini when the much faster 997 became available. She was certainly the best female rally driver of the period, but was also one of the best rally drivers without qualification. With Ann Wisdom beside her, she entered for the Monte Carlo rally at the beginning of 1962 and came seventh in class, which was a fine achievement. But five months later the two women did better and won the Tulip Rally outright, the first international rally win for the 'Min'.

The 997 and 997S Coopers continued winning rallies for several years to come, but in 1963 attention turned to the bigger Cooper 1071S. The cylinder bores were enlarged. The middle two were moved

closer together and the outer two further apart, necessitating a completely redesigned engine. The oil pump owed more to Formula Two than to Morris Minor, while valve materials were excitingly exotic at the time. The new engine gave 70bhp, a 15bhp increase, at 6000rpm, which was necessary if competition success was to continue. The engineers also managed to make the wheel rims wider, so that more rubber was on the road, and offsetting meant that bigger disc brakes with better air flow could be squeezed in.

Rauno Aaltonen was graphically described as the 'Flying Finn'. As a younger man he had won races on motorbikes, on both track and road, and in speedboats, but was soon winning rallies. Whilst Pat Moss was

Below: Paddy Hopkirk and his red Mini won the Monte Carlo Rally in 1964. Paddy went on to become a household name, while his co-driver, the late Henry Liddon, went on to become competition manager for Toyota Team Europe.

Right: 33 EJB still turns up at Mini reunion events, and is in excellent condition despite its arduous life .

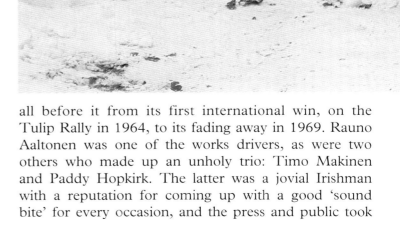

winning the Tulip, Aaltonen was coming seventh in a 997 on the RAC Rally, a result that probably didn't please him at all. The following year he was driving a 1071cc Mini and scored the factory's first major win with it on the prestigious Alpine Rally, in competition with a horde of factory and private Minis. Two years later, in a 1275S, he went on to score the only Mini victory on the RAC Rally.

The 1275S spearheaded the wins in the glory years of the mid-Sixties. Originally a lot of executives had been worried by the fact that a basic 850cc block could not be taken out to nearly 1300cc (a racing category) but company chairman George Harriman, after being harassed by John Cooper, said, 'You bloody well can!', and it was. The longer stroke necessary made this the biggest Mini a bit of a vibrator. Even at this size, the aerodynamics made it almost impossible to achieve more than the magic ton, 100mph, while anything over about 90mph set up the sort of vibration that causes mechanical and dental damage. In a rally car, of course, the parts were strengthened to cope, and the driver simply kept his mouth grimly shut for the duration of the event.

But it was a devastatingly effective tool, sweeping

all before it from its first international win, on the Tulip Rally in 1964, to its fading away in 1969. Rauno Aaltonen was one of the works drivers, as were two others who made up an unholy trio: Timo Makinen and Paddy Hopkirk. The latter was a jovial Irishman with a reputation for coming up with a good 'sound bite' for every occasion, and the press and public took

to him more than than they did to the Scandinavians, brilliant drivers though they undoubtedly were. Hopkirk was an aggressive driver, hunched bulkily over the wheel, the interior seeming too small for his furious concentration, let alone the navigator calling out pace notes beside him. He never mastered left-foot braking, unlike his team-mates who brought the tech-

nique to England, but he scored as many international works victories as Makinen (six), although they both trailed behind the nine victories of Aaltonen.

However, in the popular imagination Hopkirk is always the victor. The Mini is always red and white, festooned with a bank of spot and foglamps over the grille, screaming through a muddy, tree-strewn stage,

Above left: Timo Makinen and Paul Easter on their way to victory in their Cooper S on the Monte Carlo Rally in 1965, making it two years running for the Mini.
Above right: Rauno Aaltonen and Tony Ambrose the same year, *en route* to winning the RAC Rally. Note the sump guard – about to come in for some serious work.

the car flicking and darting, in the air, crunch, tyres scrabbling for grip as the low sump guard gouges into the track, the tail jiggling sideways as the driver pushes it out to line up for a breathless, flat-out blast down a slippery mountain pass. And that pass always leads to Monte Carlo.

Even in their prime the cars were simply modified production cars, not mid-engined four-wheel drive

Below: Competition manager Stuart Turner reads the riot act to the class of '66. From left to right: Paul Easter, Simo Lampinen, Mike Wood, Rauno Aaltonen, Tony Fall, Paddy Hopkirk, Timo Makinen, Henry Liddon and Ron Crellin.

specials like today. In international rallies they ran in Group 2 as modified cars since they obviously differed from the base models from which they were taken. By now there were Minis of every capacity and every configuration in any rally worth competing in, a veritable horde of swarming little terrors swamping the might and bulk of bigger factories with bigger cars. Overrun and demoralized, the other teams tended to question the legality of the Minis, desperate to find some excuse for being beaten by something half the size. Nevertheless, Minis won the Monte Carlo Rally, the largest and most prestigious in the world, two years running in 1964 and 1965.

The company benefited enormously from rallying success, and after Paddy Hopkirk won the Monte in 1964 the competition department could pretty much have whatever it asked for. Success meant sales, and even the grey company men could see the advantage

of helping crazy Irishmen and Finns thrash the company products into the ground – as long as they won. With the possibility of a hat-trick victory on the Monte in 1966 everyone agreed to give it whatever was necessary to win.

This was fortunate because the Monegasque organizers were far from keen to see the English sweep the board again. The usual system of handicapping, which ensured that a car from any group could theoretically win, was swept into the Mediterranean, replaced with rules that favoured Group 1 cars – virtually production cars with a run of 5000 examples made in the previous 12 months. It seems incredible now, but Stuart Turner, competition manager, managed to have production speeded up just to homologate the car for the rally. By the time of the rally just over the magic 5000 had been made. The works team was going for outright victory for the third time.

Left: The full Monte. Timo Makinen sliding his way to victory on the 1966 Monte Carlo Rally ahead of team mates Aaltonen and Hopkirk. Minis taking the first three places was too much for the officials, however, who managed to disqualify all three cars for headlamp irregularities.

Below: The 1966 RAC Rally and Tony Fall displaying high speed brinkmanship – will he or won't he?

Throughout the gruelling rally the works Minis of Makinen, Aaltonen and Hopkirk fought their way through competitors and red tape. All three were furious at their treatment and all the more determined to win. They battled through night and day, heat and rain, valley and mountain, while all the time the clock ticked away. Makinen won, then Aaltonen came second, then Hopkirk managed to squeeze ahead of the works Fords to make it third – a clean sweep for BMC and its mighty Mini. All three cars underwent intense scrutiny for over eight hours: officials went over them with tape measure and rule book, determined to find something wrong. After dismantling the engine and stripping the bodywork they eventually decided that the dipped pattern of the headlamps did not conform to the rules (they were set up for mainbeam only, the foglamps being used as dipped headlamps), and they gave victory to a Citroen. All three Minis were finally disqualified.

Naturally there was uproar, and a run-off was arranged between a standard car and the race one,

with Timo Makinen and a French journalist switching from car to car to highlight any differences. In the event the standard car actually posted a quicker time, which must have pleased Cooper S owners who now knew that their road car was quicker than Paddy Hopkirk's! Naturally the racing car was rally worn, but it gives an insight into the relative paucity of horsepower that the rally men had to play with – certainly far less than in many standard family saloons in the high street.

The following year, 1967, with no less than five works Minis out for revenge, Rauno Aaltonen won the Monte, finally gaining that longed-for hat-trick. The

Left and below: Works Minis from the 1967 season. The highlight of the season was LBL 6D winning the Monte Carlo Rally. Rauno Aaltonen and Henry Liddon got revenge for the disqualification of the previous year.
Right: 1967 Monte Carlo Rally preparation at the Abingdon workshop, where so many success stories started, was eventually closed in 1970. Tony Fall's car (foreground) finished in tenth place.

same year Paddy Hopkirk won the Alpine Rally, which proved to be the last international outright victory for the 1275S. The cars carried on, but the opposition was catching up fast. The works Porsches in particular, with 200bhp to lay down when the going was good, simply overpowered the gallant Minis, which could only keep up with manic driving in poor conditions. The last works Mini was second on the 1970 Scottish.

Although Minis continued to compete and win in private hands, the time had come for purpose-built rally cars, from Ford, Lancia and Porsche amongst others. The supremely efficient mechanics, managers and assorted personnel carried on until the axe fell on the entire department in 1970, an axe clumsily wielded by Lord Stokes who had to deal with a mob of British Leyland strikers, and the pressures of lawyers and accountants. From now on the only red bricks flying would be between strikers and management.

Above: The 1968 Monte Carlo Rally saw the Mini's dominance finally broken. Porsches finished first and second with the Minis third, fourth and fifth.

Below: Keith Baud and Mike Smith on the 1986 Rallye d'Antibes, the last international event for the 1275GT. They finished a valiant last.

Bottom: Historic rallying brings it all back. The 1990 RAC International Historic Rally was won by a replica works Mini Cooper driven by the real Timo Makinen.

Main picture: Paddy Hopkirk on the 1967 Alpine Rally, the Mini's last international competition victory.
Inset, top left: By 1967 Lucas fuel-injection was added to try to keep the 200bhp Porsches at bay but it was not sufficient to stop the inevitable decline in the face of the over whelming power advantage of the new breed of rally cars.
Inset, centre: Paddy Hopkirk uses his Irish ingenuity to keep his Mini going on the 1967 Acropolis Rally. He went on to win with Ron Crellin as his co-driver.
Inset, above: Rauno Aaltonen and his car for the 1967 Safari Rally. Aaltonen was the most successful of the works drivers, with nine international victories.

THE MONEY BOX ENIGMA

THE ARRIVAL OF THE MINI GOT THE SPECTATORS OUT OF THE SALOON BAR TO WATCH THE SALOON CAR RACING

INSTEAD. AMID THE FLEET OF GIANT SALOONS THE MINIS SWERVED AND DODGED, CUTTING INSIDE, DRIFTING

SIDEWAYS AND NIPPING THROUGH TINY GAPS BETWEEN MONSTROUS FORD GALAXIES AND JAGUARS. CARS OF

TWICE THE SIZE AND POWER WERE LEFT LUMBERING BEHIND AS THE JOYOUS MINIS ROMPED TO THE FLAG

FIRST FOR SEASON AFTER SEASON. BUT VICTORY ON THE TRACK AND CAR SALES IN THE MILLIONS STILL DID NOT

MAKE THE FACTORY THE MONEY IT WAS LOOKING FOR. THIS PARTICULAR MONEY BOX STAYED FIRMLY SHUT

UNTIL ONLY A FEW YEARS AGO, AND THE FACTORY HAD ONLY ITSELF TO BLAME.

Left: The Cooper Car Company added little luxuries such as a sun roof to the road-going version of their racer.
Above: Tennis star Ilie Nastase with a Mini City, which had sound-deadening panels to cut the racket.
Nastase would have needed more than that.

The perennial joy of the Mini is that it is so adaptable. A Mini can accommodate anywhere between one and 24 people – though not necessarily any of them in comfort – it can be raced, rallied, autotested, dragged or hillclimbed, and the chances are that the cheeky little grille and headlamps will appear at the flag first.

While the rally cars were slaying Goliaths in the dirt, other Minis were slaughtering the competition on tarmac. John Surtees sat behind the wheel of an 850 Mini as early as 1960, and Minis have continued to win saloon car races right up to the present day. Such a record of saloon car success over a period of more than 30 years makes the Mini unique. In the 1960s the main competition came from Ford Anglias – and when was the last time you saw one of those winning a race or zipping jauntily down the high street?

In the early Sixties there were Minis being raced by the factory as well as by private teams and John Cooper – all pushing and shoving to get the budgets and the victories. The end result, of course, is that

Right: South African John Love, who won the 1962 British Saloon Car Championship, in conversation with John Cooper. In the ensuing years John Cooper got to see an awful lot of trophies, from rallies, like the Monte Carlo, and road races like the Touring Car Championship.

Above: An interesting manoeuvre as Peter Harper gets hooked up with Christabel Carlisle. It happened at Silverstone in 1963 when Harper's Sunbeam Rapier got badly out of shape and ended up collecting Carlisle's Cooper S on the way to the run-off area. Sneaking past this scene, with eyes averted, is Paddy Hopkirk.

Minis triumphed, whether in factory or private livery or in the distinctive British racing green with white bonnet stripes of the Cooper Car Company. Cooper had the support of engineer Daniel Richmond in saloon car racing as well as rallying. Richmond's expertise dovetailed beautifully with the racing skills of the Cooper drivers, such as English baronet Sir John Whitmore, and South African John Love, who won the British saloon car championship in 1962.

But things did not go all Cooper's way because of the sheer breadth of ability in the saloon car field. Largely due to the determination of founder Ralph Broad, the Broadspeed team in the early Sixties could amass a wealth of driving and engineering talent to enable it to take on teams with far greater budgets.

Broad's cars were always well prepared, even over-engineered to ensure a finish, while his drivers included John Handley. John became one of the first people to compete in a Mini when he bought one the day it appeared on the local showroom floor and rallied it that afternoon. By 1963 he was racing Minis on the track as part of Team Broadspeed, alongside drivers like John Fitzpatrick, Jeff May and Peter Tempest, harrying any other Mini or competitor within striking distance.

By 1964 Cooper had picked up the contract to run the works cars in the British market, while Broad carried on racing at home and abroad, driving the cars himself and also using a tubby Irishman, Paddy Hopkirk. By the end of the season Broad's efforts were leading to financial ruin, in spite of a remarkably effective team effort. However, all was not lost for Minis that year because Warwick Banks, by then running a successful tuning business, won the European Touring Car Championship at the end of the season in his 970 Cooper S – was nowhere safe?

Left: Four cars all attempting to corner as quickly as possible, each of them taking up a different attitude, some being less in control than others. Minis can be extremely forgiving, even being pushed beyond the limits of adhesion. The Crystal Palace circuit in south London, where this action took place, is no longer in use.

Left: Minis in giant-killing form at Druids, Brands Hatch. Even massive Ford Falcons were fair game for the nimble Minis.

The following year Cooper employed a 38-year-old driver called John Rhodes, a quiet and modest man who became a holy terror once behind the wheel – he earned his nickname of 'Smokey' Rhodes the hard way. Having raced in Formula Three against such talents as Jackie Stewart, Rhodes found saloon car racing relatively easy: 'I just went flat out all the time.' You could always tell when Rhodes was approaching, since the entry to the corner would be marked by a huge cloud of smoke and dust, out of which a Mini would shoot sideways with smoke pouring off the wheels. He was the leading exponent of four-wheel drift, scrubbing the tyres sideways to knock off speed and to help line him up for the next straight. Competitors behind were often so alarmed by the sight, glimpsed through a haze of tyre smoke, of a car slewing sideways immediately in front of them, that they would back off, only to find that rather than witnessing an accident, they were, in fact, watching John Rhodes gain an even larger lead.

Theoretically, all the Minis were trying to beat the works Anglias of Mike Young and Chris Craft, but more often than not it was Broadspeed against Cooper, Fitzpatrick against Rhodes. Eventually Ralph Broad gave up the unequal financial struggle and joined the opposition, gaining instant revenge when

Right: Bigger doesn't necessarily mean better. 'Smokey' John Rhodes, in his 'born-again' ex-rally Cooper S, takes a cheeky inside line at Druids hairpin to pass a more powerful works BMW 2002ti during the 1969 Touring Car Championship event at Brands Hatch.

Below: 1969 saw the competition workshop at Abingdon (by this time part of British Leyland) preparing Minis for the track, some of them being converted from rally specification.

Bottom: A Broadspeed Escort TC at Mallory Park has a mirror-full of Minis, and probably a windscreen-full as well. John Rhodes and Steve Neal head the chase.

John Fitzpatrick, who had gone with him, won the title in 1966 with a Broadspeed Ford Anglia.

As in rallying, the competition caught up, even though the Minis kept getting faster. With Anglias, Cortinas and Escorts snapping at their exhaust pipes, the little Minis started to sweat under the pressure. The A-series engine could just about manage 140bhp, thanks to eight ports, fuel injection and boring out to 1293cc from 1275, but the power train was fairly antique and absorbed a lot of power.

Then there was the problem posed by the 10inch wheels, which simply broke at first and later caused the tyres to overheat. While larger tyres on rival vehicles ran cooler, the little Dunlops on Minis just couldn't cope with the heat caused by their small size. Switching over to 12inch wheels in 1969 helped, but by then it was largely too late.

Despite the problems, Minis simply refused to give up. Before long the 1300cc crown became unobtainable, but the 1-litre prize stayed within reach for longer. Alec Poole took the RAC saloon car championship in 1969 with his Arden-prepared 1-litre Mini, the same year that Richard Longman beat off a huge Ford Falcon to take his Mini Cooper S over the line in the first-ever race televised in colour. Longman and his Minis went on winning for some time, even securing the Group 1 RAC saloon car championship in 1978, when Group 1 was hardly the normal preserve of tiddlers like the Mini. It seemed frankly beyond belief that the little box scuttling around between all the big boys in their Escorts and Capris could possibly win, but Longman proved once again, nearly 20 years after it was established for the first time, that you should never under-estimate the Mini.

Left: This Mini was bought as a write-off and extensively rebuilt with a budget of £50. Drivers Paul Hutton, Richard Ferris and Bob Jones won the ARCO championship and several other trophies in it (despite a major crash enforcing makeshift repairs) and, more importantly, they had a great time virtually for free.

Below: Jonathan Buncombe driving a Richard Longman-prepared 1293cc Austin Cooper S at Mallory Park in 1972, a much more serious affair.

Club racers have done wonderful things with the original box, unhindered by such strict regulations, running lightweight chassis with space-frame technology, hugely wide slicks and 175bhp Ford Cosworth BDA engines. Supersaloons, British Leyland Challenge for 1275GTs, the Mini Seven Club, all of these and others have kept the Mini marque racing and, sometimes, winning – particularly in the one-marque events.

Rallycross was another area where the low centre of gravity and a wheel at each corner counted for more than outright horsepower. John Rhodes was often in the thick of things here, as well as on the track. Although his style of driving produced less smoke in rallycross, it was perfectly suited to the rough terrain, as the Minis scrabbled for grip on mud and rock. Being small, the Minis tended to almost disappear

Above: The extremely short length of a Mini hardly made it ideal for drag racing, but Gordon Jones' Mini van was highly successful on the British drag strips. BMC were originally nervous at boring the Mini engine out to 1275cc, so heaven knows what they would have made of this, since under the bonnet squats a 4.6 litre Chevrolet V8.

Right top: Randy Unsbee regularly beat more powerful competition in Sports Car Club of America C production class. High engine temperature forced him back to second place at the end of this endurance race at Gainsville, Florida. (Roger Penske also drove Minis with great enthusiasm in the Sixties before turning to Formula 1 and

under the mud of winter meetings, but that suspicious blot on the landscape often reached the chequered flag first. Perhaps a less glamorous form of off-track competition than rallycross, autocross was also a pastime at which the Mini excelled.

The Mini survived on the race track rather longer than it did on the rally circuits, where it was effectively

CART involvement.) Federal government safety and emissions standards for 1968 caused BMC to stop exporting to the U.S. on economic grounds. Then in the mid-Seventies the SCCA changed its rules, effectively outclassing the racing version.

Right, second from top: Long-time Mini exponent Richard Longman with his 1275GT Clubman at Brands Hatch in 1978. That year, long after the Mini had ceased to be considered competitive, he won the Group1 RAC British Saloon Car Championship. Longman has supplied engines for customers in Germany, Sweden, and in America where it won for its owner the SCCA national championship.

Right, third from top: Nowhere in the world is the Mini more desired than in the Land of the Rising Sun, where the Mini's heritage and compact dimensions make it a prized possession. Cars are preferred to be in as original a state as possible — note the Leyland Team sun strip still in place on the left-hand car.

Right: Although this Mini Miglia racer is not particularly old, it has a period-style race seat with external frame. The interior is purely functional, all original equipment being replaced by bare essentials for safety, driver comfort and instrumentation. At this level of competition race cars are clinical environments.

Not many cars can compete in virtually every category of motorsport there is.

Above: Lose weight and you'll fly. This rallycross Mini has shed its one-piece front body-work somewhere but is still in the running... or the flying.

Right: Trying hard to stay ahead, let alone on the circuit, the driver's forward vision is restricted to the 'letter-box' slot in the perspex windscreen. Here's mud in your eye!

Below: Space-framed Maguire Minis proved giantkillers in the special saloon categories of circuit racing and hill climbs in the 1970s as Phil Crouch demonstrated at Prescott's Pardon hairpin in April 1984.

finished after about 1970. This was partly due to British Leyland keeping up some sort of grudging support for the racing programme, whereas the rally workshop at Abingdon was reduced to carrying out commercial tuning work. Individual enthusiasm or professional team entries are all very well, but you can only expect so many miracles without ground support from the factory, and after Lord Stokes took control backing became increasingly patchy.

One of the problems was that the marketing men seem to have been slow to grasp the sales potential of speed. The original Mini Cooper generated far more sales than they were prepared for, while they were sure that the S would basically be a homologation special, used almost exclusively for racing. But, of course, peo-ple instantly went out and flaunted their S badges on the road. The 997 and 1275cc engines were obviously aimed at the 1-litre and 1300cc competition classes, but the 1275S proved to be the most popular with the man in the street, selling something in the region of 40,000 units, which was far beyond what the marketing men imagined.

There have always been anomalies about the Mini, from its inception to the present day. There is no real reason why the Mini should still be in production, apart from the fact that it would appear that Rover actually make money from producing it. This is a relatively new state of affairs since for many years, when spare parts are taken into the equation, Minis were built and sold either at a loss or just for a small profit.

It seems absurd that a car as popular as the Mini, which passed five million sales in 1986, could not have made a fortune, but the problems go back to the launch in 1959. There was no real pricing structure at BMC in those days, which seems strange by today's standards when most companies are run by accountants. It seems probable that the Mini was priced at its launch value of £496 simply because that under-cut the Ford Anglia of the day. At first that cheap price actually put some people off since they imagined anything the cost of a Ford Popular would have the same level of primitive engineering, little realizing that they were ignoring the bargain of the century. When later Mini models came along the company compounded the error by basing their price structure on that of the original Mini.

The management, in true British fashion, tended to come up from the shop floor since this was traditionally seen as the proper path to follow. Graduates and bright academics were mistrusted, so any radical ideas they may have had seldom got more than a negative grunt from the Midlands management. None of this was conducive to new ideas or modern business practices, so by the time Lord Stokes took over what was then BLMC in 1968 he inherited nearly 50 factories scattered all over the country, with the consequent communication problems and high transport costs between parts of the empire. The factories themselves were chronically overmanned by a workforce enfeebled by restrictive union agreements that crippled output

Above left and right: The long production run of the Mini has seen many changes. Early production lines, shown here, had to give way to more modern processes, until the Mini eventually shared Metro lines, with considerable savings in time and money.
Left: Crash testing used to be carried out by the owners, but is now scientifically done by the factory.
Below left: Quaint, by modern methods, these left-hand drive models are loaded on to a Bristol Freighter for their European destination.
Below: Export markets demand different specifications such as the American-style bumpers on this Canadian example.
Right: How it was, and how it stayed. A British Leyland Mini saloon from 1978 shows the timeless shape that first appeared in 1959. It is highly unlikely that the shape will change again, with production projected at least until the end of the century.

and stifled discussion.

It wasn't until 1977 that the then Leyland Cars instigated a computer accounting system that told the management whether their cars were making a profit or a loss. Computer analysis revealed that the Mini was making a loss. During the following years painful battles with the unions and the company's own improved methods of production and accountancy slowly started to turn things round. The workforce had gone up considerably, but this was not without some justification since the added complexity of the Mini compared to the early models – with new Minis having heaters and dual-circuit brakes and so on – meant that more workers were needed to make one car. Nevertheless, it was accepted that the company was at least 35 per cent over-manned and the whittling down

process was both painful and expensive.

The lack of profit from the car also meant that there had been little investment, and it has always been known that to revamp the Mini would cost a prohibitive amount of money. There simply wasn't much that could be done apart from making it cheaper through implementing better working methods with a smaller workforce. The Mini will always be expensive to make compared to more modern cars because there are so many seams, turns and nuts and bolts.

Now Rover Cars are said to make a profit on every Mini they make, although the old adage that small cars make small profits would certainly seem to hold true in the case of Rover's smallest money box. It's just a shame that it took nearly 30 years for even this to come true.

TWINI MINI AND OTHER MUTANTS

THESE DAYS A DARING CAR MANUFACTURER ADDS A FOUR-WHEEL DRIVE SYSTEM OR AN ESTATE BODY TO A HIGH-SELLING CAR, BUT IN THE PAST BMC WOULD HAVE A GO AT ANYTHING. THE MINI SPAWNED A WHOLE FAMILY OF ODD-BALLS, FROM THE FUNKY MOKE TO THE WACKY TWINI MINI. SPECIALIST BUILDERS SOON GOT IN ON THE ACT, ADDING BODYWORK AND EXTRAS TO MAKE SOME VERY DISTANT RELATIVES OF THE ORIGINAL MINI - SOME BEAUTIFUL OFFSPRING, BUT ALSO SOME THAT SEEMED RATHER INBRED. ONE CAN ONLY SPECULATE ABOUT THE EMBRYONIC PLANS THAT WERE NEVER BORN.

Left: Surf's up! Mokes are now imported to Britain from Portugal. In 1966 twenty Mokes, customized for Capitol Records by George Barris, were Beach Boys radio competition prizes. The Beach Boys had Mokes too.
Above: The Mini dog, a fur-covered creation, at the 30th birthday celebrations at Silverstone in 1989.

Lately Rover have been content to churn out Minis merely with different badges and paint schemes, but back in the Sixties BMC had the courage to experiment with genuine alternatives. Their range of options in body shape and engine specification stands up well in comparison to the output of the Nineties – how many Metro variants are there, for instance?

There may have been management problems in the disparate British Leyland corporation of the Seventies, but when they started, BMC were eager to make as many Mini variations as possible. There were the obvious ones like the estate version and the Clubman, which had more space under the bonnet at the expense of style and aerodynamics, but there were many others that never saw production, like two attempts to make a Mini sports car to replace the MG

Midget: the MG Mini and Michelotti Mini.

Better known, even though they never gained popularity in the UK, were the Italian Innocenti Minis, which were smart Bertone-styled hatchbacks that sold well in Italy. The factory was later sold to entrepreneur Alejandro De Tomaso, who kept the shape but replaced the A-series engine with Daihatsu blocks – when is a Mini not a Mini?

Back in Britain came the Riley Elf and Wolseley Hornet, two models that stretched and beautified the original Mini with boot extensions, plusher grille and smarter interior. BMC sold 59,000 of these during the Sixties, presumably to people who wanted something slightly more refined than the basic box of tricks.

BMC certainly had a stab at filling every every niche in the market. On the one hand they catered for

The Mini was used as a basis for all sorts of projects, including the two shown here to replace the MG Midget. **Above:** This MG Mini carries the MG octagon on the grille, but is still unmistakeably Mini. **Below:** The Michelotti Mini had a Targa-type roof and styling by the famous Italian house. Built on a 1275GT base in 1970, this prototype was too heavy, and the cost of de-toxing the engine for the important American market proved uneconomic, so ADO 70 was shelved.

the dodderers in their respectable Rileys, and on the other they made the Mini Moke, a car without any reason for being except for fun – as if the normal Mini wasn't fun enough to start with. The Moke was an attempt to produce a lightweight military vehicle that could be parachuted into action, but its low ride height meant that it wasn't really suitable for rough terrain and instead it headed for an easier life in the leisure market. It served happily on beaches, golf courses and anywhere hot, although Mokes with hoods and plastic screens could sometimes be seen squelching round English roads, driven by soggy, fun-loving owners. Tooling was sold off to the Australians in the late Sixties but by the Eighties production had re-started in Portugal, with vehicles being imported back into England, to revive memories of the Swinging Sixties.

The popularity of the Moke was enhanced by its regular appearances in the television series 'The Prisoner'. It also led to a more serious, if seriously worrying, development, the Twini Moke. This was the brainchild of Issigonis himself, who thought that it would be a neat idea to add another engine in the back to go with the one in the front. John Cooper became an enthusiastic advocate of the principle, and it wasn't long before a Twini Mini with 175bhp on tap from a total of 2.5 litres was entered for racing. It was a novel idea but not totally satisfying from an engineering point of view since both engines acted completely independently, each powering one set of wheels. The only connections between the two were the throttle cables and two gear levers clamped together.

As could be expected, the Twini handled rather

Left: A highly modified German Leyland Motor Sports racing version of the Italian Innocenti Mini, built under licence from Britain.

Below: The Innocenti Mini was produced in Italy from 1974 to '82 and still looks surprisingly modern. The hatchback and clean lines pre-date the Metro by six years and in 1982 the wheezing A-series engine was replaced by a Daihatsu unit, bringing the car bang up to date. Not bad for something based on a 1959 design.

Above: The MG M-Type was in a limbo between the Mini and the Riley Elf / Wolsley Hornet derivatives. **Above right:** The Guy Salmon Special was another attempt to create a sporting image, this time based on the Clubman, utilising an MG 1100 grille.

Right: An Austin-badged alternative to the Moke, driven by Sir Alec Issigonis himself, who must have wondered just how far the original design could be pushed. This is a fun vehicle for beaches or golf courses, and uses the Elf/Hornet boot. The Morris-badged beach car (to its right) stuck to the more conventional, but smaller load-carrying, boot of the Mini.

Above and right: The twin-engined Mini Moke was Issigonis' personal project, although John Cooper developed the idea to build a Twini-Mini. Aimed at military use the twin engines, linked only by throttles and gear levers, left no room for kit.

strangely, but the racing Twini was capable of spinning all four wheels and setting faster times than a single-engined version so long as the driver got used to the rather odd cornering. None really succeeded in racing, and since the engines took up a lot of space there wasn't any other particular application for which they were suited. John Cooper, however, remained a committed enthusiast, even after one broke its steering when he was hurtling down the Kingston by-pass, south of London. In the ensuing accident he fractured his skull, but even this doesn't seem to have knocked the idea of a Twini Mini or Moke out of his head. Ironically it was an original Mini part which had failed

and had nothing to do with the twin-engined set-up.

Needless to say, it was not left entirely up to the factory to tinker around with ideas. One of the major Mini advantages is that the engine has its own sub-frame, so a power-pack can easily be taken from one car and added to another. For the last 30 years Mini

Above left: The 1974 SRV4 project car was an attempt to make the Mini safer, a thoroughly boring project and result. The wheelbase was longer, to improve crushability, and the front was lowered and softened to hurt pedestrians less if they walked in front of it. The interior was like a padded cell, and was as much fun to be in.

Above: In 1975, in semi-retirement, Issigonis worked on a gearless Mini project. The bodywork was part of an earlier exercise, but the interest lay under the bonnet, with a 1500cc overhead camshaft engine designed to run with a variable automatic transmission similar to the DAF system. In the event the project was shelved.

Above: Although never intended for competition, this Moke was entered in the 1977 London to Sydney Marathon. The 'roo bars' came in useful in London to deter over-enthusiastic enthusiasts, and were essential in Australia to deflect errant kangaroos.

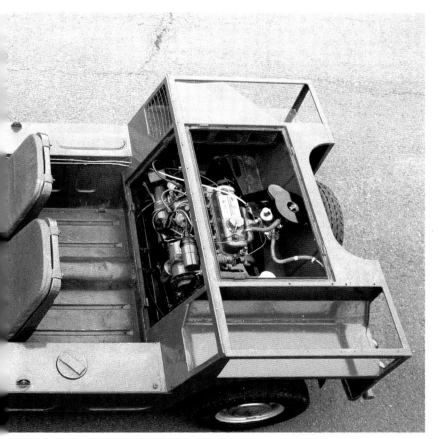

parts have been cheap, effective and available, all admirable qualities for those who wanted to put small-scale small cars into production. It should be remarked that many of them appear to have been designed by engineers who never had an art education, the results showing just how 'right' the original design was all

those years ago.

The first thing that many people did to a small, low car was to make it lower still. Effectively, you chain-saw horizontally through the bodywork and through the window pillars and then weld the sections together again, remembering to lower the seat, unless you like surgical collars. Both the Arden Mini Sprint, which was inspired by Mini tuning guru Clive Trickey, and the Broadspeed GT went this route, the Mini Sprint losing three inches between floorpan and roof, the Broadspeed five. The latter also had a fast-back fitted, which helped weight and aerodynamics to produce a car noticeably faster than stock. Private individuals

INTRODUCING THE BROADSPEED G.T. 2 + 2

BROADSPEED are proud to present their revolutionary G.T. 2 + 2, which gives an exciting and unforgettable experience in motoring. These cars are for the motorist to whom driving is an essential part of his day to day life, but likes to do it with flair and who enjoys the supreme pleasure of a car which gives the ultimate in control and response, combined with the looks of a thoroughbred. Naturally, we have not forgotten the requirements of the racing enthusiast, to whom the word "Broadspeed" is synonymous with the tough and competitive world of international saloon car racing.

In these models lie the culmination of experiments conducted by the top engineers in our competition department and the gruelling test of world famous race tracks.

Don't take our word for it. Come and see for yourself. Admire the gleaming body, the interior, fitted and finished by craftsmen and finally examine the superb engineering and you will understand why Broadspeed are proud to present their . . . . . .

MINI MARCOS GT

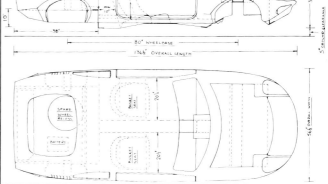

also chose this path, sawing away with gay abandon, to produce cars radically lower than stock, suitable only for posing in by persons of restricted growth.

The Mini Marcos is perhaps the best known of the Mini variants, since it has been in production, on and off, since 1965. Marcos Cars built winning GT racers in the early Sixties and went on to make a fibre-glass-bodied special using Mini mechanicals. This was not a back-street bodge but a pukka racing tool – in 1966 it was the only British car to finish the 24-hour race at Le Mans. Forays into other models led to disaster but sales of the Marcos stayed steady over the years, even though the moulds were sold on to several other companies before Marcos Cars bought the

moulds back and started up production again.

The Midas was developed from the Marcos and was probably the better car. The range culminated in the Midas Gold coupe, running mostly Metro components, with the faithful A-series engine. The chassis design, which was partly fashioned by Formula One guru Gordon Murray, featured under-body ground effect, which helped the little car stick to the road like an F1 car. Some of these Mini derivatives may not have looked beautiful, but their allure certainly went more than skin-deep.

The GTM goes back almost as far as the Marcos, to 1969. This was an enclosed two-seater sports car model, with the A-series engine in the middle driving

Opposite top left: The Broadspeed GT was designed by tuning guru Ralph Broad in the Sixties, and was one of the first to cut and chop. Five inches came off the height, while the fast-back treatment improved aerodynamics and weight reduction to the point where the car was often faster than the Cooper. **Opposite top right:** Also developed through competition, the Stewart & Ardern Mini was chopped by three inches and de-seamed to produce a more wind-cheating shape.

Below left: The Mini Marcos was one of the first Mini kit-cars. The wheelbase was longer than the stock Mini and it was simple to assemble, using Mini front and rear sub-frames attached to a fibre-glass monocoque body. Production has restarted with a lot of interest in Japan. **Bottom left:** Driver and constructor Jem Marsh proved the worth of the Marcos aerodynamics in practice for the 1967 Le Mans 24-hour race when he was clocked at 141mph along the Mulsanne straight using nothing more than a rally spec engine. The previous year a Marcos was the only British finisher.

Below right: A Mini Jem, an 'interim Marcos' produced by Jem Marsh whilst the Marcos company was inactive, hustles round the Nurburgring's Karussell.

Bottom right: Too expensive to produce economically the Unipower was made for only four years. The mid-engined design stood at only 41 inches high.

Above: Industrial designer David Ogle created the elegant Ogle SX1000.
Below: The Mini Domino Premiere is a particularly neat convertible, the roof being replaced by a Targa-type roll-over bar with removable roof panels.

the rear wheels. Made of fibreglass, the GTM was light and sporty, with a claimed 120mph if using the 1275cc lump. It wasn't a bad looking car, if a little bug-eyed, but its rounded form compared favourably to that of the Mini Status. This was designed by Brian Luff who used to work at Lotus and John Frayling, who did design work on the Lotus Elite. The body is finished in self-coloured orange fibreglass – such an orange wedge may be different to the more buxom curves of the Mini, but it's hard to say that it looks anything like as good. It's much easier to say it looks horrible!

The Unipower was another odd shape, again with

a goofy bonnet that came out well beyond the drive wheels. In its favour was a light weight, some four hundredweight less than a standard Cooper S. This naturally did wonders for its performance, particularly when allied to one of the larger and hairier Mini engines, which would sit amidships in the tubular steel chassis covered in fibreglass. Some racing success followed, although the car went out of production in 1970 after only four years in production.

The Ogle Mini isn't too misnamed. After some of the other designs around it looks rounded, complete, well thought out. In fact, the creator, David Ogle, was a professional designer, who designed a range of Bush radios at about the same time as the SX1000 Ogle came out. It was fairly expensive, since the body cost as much as a Cooper, but it gave good value for money. Intelligently, the original body was taken off at bumper level and a GRP body was then grafted on, so all of the floorpan, wheelarches and so on were standard and strong. Weight was a little more than for a stock Cooper but the improved aerodynamics gave a useful increase in top speed.

Saloon car racer John Whitmore bought one and made some publicity for the company, but even so Ogle only sold about 70 models before he was killed in a road accident in one of his own machines.

There were many other wacky specials, including single-seaters like the Mini Midget, racers like the

Above: The Midas Gold was the ultimate development of the Marcos, both designs owned at one time by Harold McDermot. The chassis was designed by Gordon Murray of McLaren Formula One fame.
Right: BMC almost built a four-wheel drive Mini. This four-wheel drive from Burundi mates a Mini body to a Suzuki SJ413 chassis.

140mph Landar and numerous Moke derivatives, including the Scamp and Jimini. Some were only produced for a year or two, others for nearly as long as the Mini has been in production. All of them sought to capitalize on the basic strengths of the Mini car, while somehow redressing some of its weaknesses. Many ended up lighter, by using fibreglass bodywork, and many ended up faster just through improved aerodynamics. It would be almost impossible to design a car with a worse drag coefficient than the Mini, but while some were more slippery, few were more attractive than the basic little box designed by Issigonis back in the Fifties.

The factory too was happy to experiment. Even as far back as 1957 BMC engineers had a list of about 15 variations of the basic Mini that they wanted to see in production and, while not all made it, many went on to become part of the burgeoning Mini family.

One of the ideas that never made it was mooted in the Sixties, and that was for a four-wheel drive version, using not two engines like in the Twini but a sophisticated drive system not dissimilar to set-ups currently

in use – the factory got as far as taking out a patent on it. That might have led to a whole mini-industry since the four-wheel drive market is one of the main growth areas left in the automotive market.

An idea of what it might have looked like can be gained from a short trip to Bujumbura in Burundi, central Africa, where a butch-looking four-wheel drive Mini is often seen skipping about the muddy tracks. In truth it is a Suzuki SJ413 chassis and engine with a Mini bodywork grafted neatly on. The owner had a Suzuki and a Mini and reckons that the combination is better than either of them separately since he now has a Mini that can cross country, while the heavier Mini

body gives a lower and more stable ride than that of the standard Suzuki off-roader. It certainly looks good, giving some idea of what might have been, and demonstrates one of the Mini's perennial joys – its adaptability. After more than five million sales, dozens of prototypes, mock-ups, working models and short-run specials from both the factory and private garages, there is still no sign that we have reached the end of the potential of the mighty Mini.

Left: It's all here; the purple metalflake paint and flame job, side exhaust, and the grille off a Vauxhall Ventora.

Opposite centre and bottom: The long and the short of it. This Dutch Mini is definitely the world's shortest since front and rear screens meet at the top. You could park it anywhere in town, but would not be able to take any shopping home with you. That is not a problem with the Mini limousine.

Right and below: How low can you go? Andy Summers, wild man of the British custom scene, definitely doesn't suffer from claustrophobia. This is the lowest road-legal car in the world, with an astonishing 17¾ inches chopped from the height of a standard Mini that he bought for £10. The main restraint on chopping the height was the shock absorbers, which he didn't want to poke through the bodywork. The roof height was determined by the physical limits imposed by the actual need for the driver to get in and be able to drive. To this end the rather natty seats are actually old garden chairs, with their legs removed, re-upholstered in white vinyl. The smoked-glass sun-roof aids forward visibility for such important items as road signs and traffic lights.

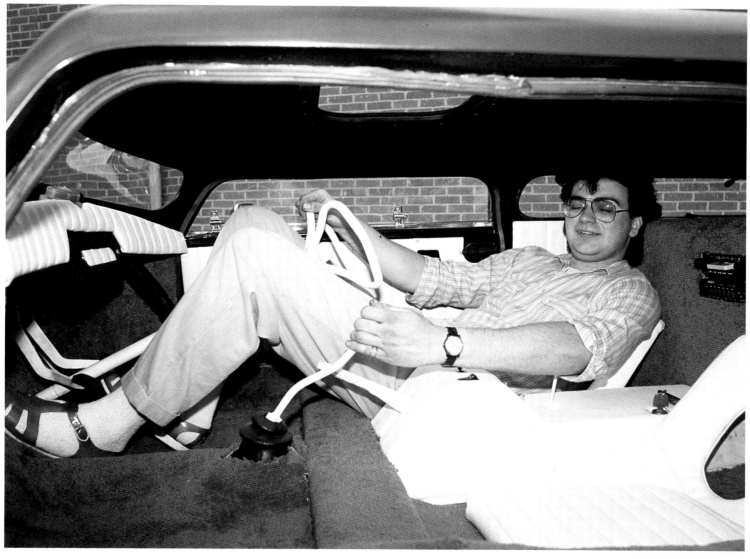

CHAPTER 6

THIRTY PLUS AND STILL IN STYLE

AFTER ALL THESE YEARS THE MINI SHOWS NO SIGNS OF SLOWING DOWN. FOR NEARLY 20 YEARS THE FACTORY AND JOHN COOPER WERE SEPARATED, BUT NOW THE ALLIANCE IS ONCE MORE IN PLACE, TURNING OUT NEW CARS AND TURNING UP BRIGHT IDEAS FOR THE FUTURE. SPECIALIST MANUFACTURERS ARE STILL MAKING MINIS OF RADICAL PERFORMANCE AND OUTRAGEOUS LUXURY, ALL TO NEW DESIGNS DESPITE THE INFLUENCE OF THE EARLIER COACH BUILDERS. THE FASHION OF THE SIXTIES IS BACK, AND THE MINI IS STILL AS RELEVANT TODAY AS IT WAS IN 1959, ONLY NOW IT'S LEAN AND GREEN.

Left: One of the many special editions produced, this one called, unsurprisingly, the Mini Chelsea.
Above: The 25th anniversary of the Mini was celebrated with this special edition finished in, of course, metallic silver paint.

The Mini should really have faded into glorious obscurity after the arrival of the Metro in 1980. Mini sales halved when the Metro was launched but, against the forecasts at Austin Rover, they didn't go into a Stuka nose-dive. There were enough sales to make it worth continuing to build the little boxes, especially as Minis now ran on Metro production lines, which were considerably more efficient than those of the 1970s. Naturally, the number of options and new models declined, until there were just two main models produced: the City and the more expensive Mayfair. That left plenty of room for the latter-day Wood and Picketts to carve expensive little niches in the Mini market.

Everything about the Mini seems to come full circle. In the Sixties the Mini box became bejewelled with carpets, wood, leather and pearlescent paint. In the late Eighties the whole thing happened again. One of the

Left: The marketing department taking an unfair advantage. The Advantage special edition of 1987 was going to be called the Wimbledon, but the parties concerned could not come to an agreement.

Below: At the other end of the spectrum is the Park Lane, a more sophisticated special.

Right: The Mini Mayfair, named after another area of London, has been continuously in the Mini line-up for more than twelve years, as other specials come and go.

main differences is that performance is now more important if you are going to have a flash car – some 'go' to back up the 'show'.

And what a show. Probably the most expensive Mini ever made is the BAC M-30, the initials standing for the British Automobile Company, who unveiled this Mini for the 30th Anniversary celebrations in 1989. This is a body-beautiful, drowned deep in pearlescent paint – a 30th anniversary being celebrated with pearls. There is no chrome, only hallmarked solid silver for the badges on the outside, while the interior contains most of a small landscape. Think of a forest of elm trees, with cows gently browsing around them. The inside of the trees and the outside of the cows now cover the inside of the M-30. The leather is from the same company, Bridge of Weir, that upholsters the Houses of Parliament, but draping leather over the two multi-adjustable seats in the M-30 seems a better use of resources than putting padded seats into the rump of Parliament.

Inside is total luxury, with a CD player and car phone to amuse (they hadn't thought of either in the Sixties or else they'd have put them in). But it's under the bonnet where the main differences lie, with not just a stock engine or even a Cooper, but a supercharged Metro motor that gives 115 – miles per hour and brake horsepower. Some of the Sixties extravaganzas could only manage about half that speed, weighed down as they were with everything from televisions to drinks cabinets. Such is progress. The M-30 continues the 30 theme since there will only be 30 made and the price tag is £30,000 – for that you could buy half a dozen Mini Citys, but that is the price of exclusivity.

On a more realistic level is the ERA, not much more than a third of the price of the M-30 yet with similar performance. Under the bonnet sits the Metro Turbo 1275cc engine. With carefully tuned suspension and uprated brakes, this is a fearsome yet neatly pack-

Above: In 1988, in a decade obsessed with designer marketing, the Mini got the designer treatment from Mary Quant, who had been a fan ever since the Sixties. The interior was predominantly black and white stripes, reminiscent of the Op Art phase.
Below left: The 1989 special editions ranged from the more feminine cars at the rear (Rose, and Sky) to the more macho Flame, and Racing, at front, with colour schemes reminiscent of the Sixties Coopers.
Below right: Yet another permutation on exterior paint, interior finish and a name tag: this time it's the Neon.

Right: A stylish Mini cabriolet built by Swift and based on the Mini 30 special edition. Compare this with the factory Cabriolet on page 77.

Below: The ERA Mini Turbo was hot, with performance coming from a tweaked Metro Turbo A-series engine. The production run of the £12,000 flier has officially ended, but some are being built for the Japanese market.

Below: The Kent Automotive Development project is a 16-valve, twin cam head to fit the ageing A-series engine. The work liberates a surprising amount of power from the old block and may feature in a future Cooper, returning with interest the power lost by heavy exhaust silencing and catalytic converters.

aged bundle of fun. The styling accentuates the chunky, child-like proportions of the car but performance is definitely adults-only. ERAs are practical tools, a balanced blend of power and handling, but the turbo lag and rev-happy nature of the beast detract from an ultimate accolade.

The finest engine to put in a Mini would appear to be that produced by KAD, Kent Automotive Developments. The now ancient and venerable A-series engine is the biggest stumbling block for those who want to drag the Mini into the next century. More particularly, it is the cylinder head, which has all the free-breathing of a terminal asthmatic, which stops power pouring out. KAD have designed their own, very high-quality twin-cam head with four valves per cylinder to get round the problem. A sophisticated Weber Alpha engine management system joins the new all-alloy head, which will take a vast array of carburation, from single SU to individual throttle butterflies for competition use. It fits, but only just, under

Left, main pic: A Rover France publicity shot for the After Eight: a quintessentially British photo setting for a Mini 'mint'.

Left, inset: Two more from France, the Mayfair on the right is the same as the UK specification but the Special on the left (and above) is known in Britain as the City.

the bonnet, and liberates a considerable number of horses. Competition engines should produce something approaching 200bhp – an almost unbelievable performance from such a small engine, which was designed as an 850cc back in the Forties.

The KAD design is so good that John Cooper himself is in talks with the company with a view to producing what could be the ultimate Cooper. 'The KAD Mini is a very well designed vehicle', he states. 'Looking to the future, it could become a very expensive, limited edition car with 115bhp. They do a first-class engineering job, and it would be nice to do one of the ultimate Minis – perhaps badged as a Mini Cooper 1.6Si.'

That is in the future, but for now John Cooper Garages Ltd has as much Mini work as at any time since the Sixties thanks to increased interest in the car and the subsequent increased production at Rover. Rover Cars are now producing about 45,000 Minis a year, after a total production run of something like five and a quarter million cars – you can't call them units. The aberration of the Clubman of the Seventies has disappeared, and we are back to the familiar rounded, cosy shape that so caught the public's imagination in the Sixties. The Mini City and Mini Mayfair are both-selling well, particularly overseas, with Japan as the biggest market. Japan buys more Minis than the UK itself or any other foreign market – last year Mini exports to Japan were around 12,000 cars. Partly as a result of Japanese interest, Rover are selling more Minis now than they were five years ago, with a product that has remained essentially unchanged for several decades.

But it is not all Mayfairs and Citys – between 40 and 50 per cent of all Mini production carries that famous name: Cooper. When Lord Stokes asked John Cooper what it was he actually did for the company

Above and right: Nowhere is the Mini more popular than in Japan. About forty per cent of all Rover's Mini production goes to the Japanese market, as well as specials, kits, and of course Coopers. It is such a major market that manufacturers produce specifically for it. The Mini's British pedigree and small size ensure cult status.

back in 1970 it was obvious that the gentleman's agreement between him and the company was about to end. During the Seventies and Eighties it seemed as if the Mini Cooper was going to be relegated to a chapter of history, but then the Japanese pressed him for a Cooper kit to be fitted to the standard cars being exported to Japan. By 1989 Minis were landing in Japan with a large and impressive box on the back seat, in which could be found all manner of Cooper goodies, including twin carbs, new head, exhaust and so on, to make up a Cooper special.

Eventually a Japanese kit appeared in England, arriving at a fortuitous time. Time, in fact, had been kind to John Cooper, who had not sat around idle since losing his links with Leyland in 1970. He now runs an award-winning Honda dealership on the English south coast, although in among the CRXs and NSXs squat old Coopers from the Monte Carlo Rally and even older single-seater racers. Time had also seen a conveyor belt of management and business methods passing through the tortured Leyland factories, a conveyor belt that moved too fast to let anyone pay much attention to the little old box in the corner that still sold steadily. By the time the John Cooper Garages Anniversary special came out the Mini was produced by Rover Cars, and the conveyor belt had slowed dramatically.

Instead of ignoring what Cooper had to offer, the

new management took a couple of examples of the new car, road-tested it for 20,000 miles on German autobahns and started offering the kit through Rover dealerships with full factory warranty. Once again, the Mini and the Cooper names were reunited and once

Above and left: The latest model from Rover is the Cabriolet converted by Lamm Autohaus, Fuchsberg, in Germany. Note that it has a full soft top unlike the other Targa-type conversions. With a wider track, full bodykit and a Cooper 1275cc engine, it is sure to be a head-turner and neck-stretcher, especially as production is limited.

on. Although the Mini is essentially the same, the Nineties have different values to the Sixties, in spite of the revival of Sixties fashions. A three-way exhaust catalyst is now standard fitment to pass more stringent emission control regulations. Unleaded fuel and a catalytic converter make the car more environmentally friendly, but they do nothing for performance. John Cooper realized that it was essential to get the 1275cc engine into the car, even though this presented problems with noise regulations.

ERA, mentioned earlier, helped with fan and exhaust noise suppression since they had built up a lot of experience when putting their Minis together. Eventually it was done but still that was not enough. The latest introduction is single-point fuel injection, to get back some more of that lost performance. The Mini is holding its place in the market and the heart, not just wallowing in nostalgia, but fighting in the market-place. John Cooper now offers a limited edition 1275S pack, with the classic ingredients of twin SU carburettors, gas-flowed cylinder head, oil cooler, high-performance exhaust (with catalytic converter) and much more. He also has a whole range of accessories, like throttle pedal, seat adjusting brackets, and all the other goodies that were so much the rage in the Sixties.

The factory is not being left out because Rover is now selling nostalgia kits for Coopers, with names like

again you could buy a Mini Cooper from the factory – or John Cooper's dealership.

But time does not stand still. Once again we have the cars, an enthusiastic factory management and the customer interest, but the cars themselves have moved

Above: Serious equipment in the shape of the new Mini Cooper 1275S complete with the master's signature on the bonnet stripes. In the background lurks 6 EMO, a brutal, noisy, and devastating £25,000's worth of replica works rally car in which Paddy Hopkirk and Alec Poole won the 1990 Pirelli Marathon in a style reminiscent of the finest moments of the Sixties.

Left: Leather trim in the latest Coopers cannot really disguise the fact that this is no limousine, and Sir Alec's dictum still holds good: the car should not be so comfortable that the driver loses concentration.

'RAC Rally Pack' and 'The Monte Carlo Pack', with spotlamps, bonnet stripes, sump guard, the works. Any Sixties Mini enthusiast would feel instantly at home.

Rover is also moving on its own account. You wouldn't have thought that there could be a new permutation on the Mini, but the factory has come up with one: the Mini Cabriolet. In Chapter Two we saw how specialist companies like Wood and Pickett made plush convertibles, but until now the factory has always fitted a hard top to its Minis. It is expensive, but it is fairly exclusive and you get Cooper running gear, monster Revolution wheels, full body kit and a slinky interior. One wonders what else the factory has up its corporate sleeve.

Above: Cooper brochure for the biggest market, Japan. It was the Japanese who demanded the Cooper performance kits in 1987, kits that eventually appeared in Europe. Were it not for the Japanese there would merely be a succession of special edition Minis. At least we now have, once again, some 'go' to match the 'show', and the Japanese have 'talking-point' cocktail cabinets converted out of the Cooper kit packing crate.

As for John Cooper, he knows what he wants next. 'Now we're looking at a twin-point fuel injection system, as opposed to the current single-point, to create more interest and performance. With the KAD car, the cabriolet, multi-point fuel injection, I think the Mini could go on until at least the end of the Nineties.' He laughs happily at the thought.

It seems incredible that the same John Cooper, whose racing cars won Formula One World Championships more than 30 years ago, and whose rally cars won virtually every international rally there is, repeatedly, can still be very much in business, planning and scheming for the future up to the end of the century. But he is not alone. The interest shown in historic rallies, with drivers racing and crashing replica historic cars, is opening up a whole new market. The Historic Rally Car Register has seen an upsurge in interest over the years until we now have huge entry lists, each car not a modern replica but a carefully restored original.

This is not a doddery sport for those with weak memories and rose-tinted glasses, but a competitive, if enjoyable, race series. Mini Coopers abound, and so do their original drivers. Timo Makinen won the RAC Rally in the series, while Paddy Hopkirk has won the Pirelli Marathon – it only remains for Rauno Aaltonen to come out of retirement and the Three Musketeers will be back on the road again, with John Cooper cheering from the sidelines, thinking up more ways of keeping the Mini and the Cooper on the road and on the track.

With sales actually increasing, with large export markets, particularly in France and Japan, with new products from an enthusiastic management and up-to-date emission controls, the Mini looks set to sail past the end of the century. When Sir Alec Issigonis designed the car back in the Fifties he wanted a cheap car for the working man, but under the enthusiastic onslaught of people like John Cooper, he slowly came to realize the potential locked up in his box. These days you will see a mum in a City, a female executive in a Cabriolet, a young gun in a Cooper 1275S and countless others in cars for the working day.

On the motorways, which were built after the Mini was designed, the Mini is uncomfortable and noisy. On back roads it is the most incredible fun; cornering like a vehicle that has no dimensions, it is merely a point. And in town it is as perfect as it ever. was. Although many have tried, nobody has replaced such a perfect package in a ten-foot box.

INDEX

Figures in *italics* refer to captions